Magnesium

A BEGINNER'S QUICK GUIDE TO HEART AND BONE HEALTH WITH A 5-STEP ACTION PLAN

Mary Golanna

copyright © 2024 Mary Golanna

All rights reserved No part of this book may be reproduced, or stored in a retrieval system, or transmitted in any form or by any means, electronic, mechanical, photocopying, recording, or otherwise, without express written permission of the publisher.

CONTENTS

Introduction v

Chapter 1. What is Magnesium? 1

Chapter 2. Understanding Magnesium Deficiency 10

Chapter 3. Use Cases of Magnesium 16

Chapter 4. Pros and Cons 21

Chapter 5. 5-Step Plan to Get Started with Magnesium ... 27

Chapter 6. Dietary Sources of Magnesium 44

Chapter 7. Sample Magnesium-Rich Recipes 49

Conclusion 67

FAQs 71

Resources and Helpful Links 75

INTRODUCTION

Magnesium is a mineral that's often overlooked, yet it plays a crucial role in our overall health and well-being. Its importance stretches far beyond what many people realize, affecting everything from our mood to our muscle function. If you've ever felt fatigued or experienced muscle cramps, the culprit might just be a lack of magnesium. But what exactly makes this mineral so vital?

In recent years, magnesium has caught the attention of health enthusiasts and researchers alike. Studies have highlighted its potential benefits, from supporting heart health to enhancing sleep quality. With such a wide range of positive effects, it's no wonder that magnesium is gaining traction in health circles.

Yet, with so much information out there, finding reliable guidance can feel overwhelming. That's where this guide steps in, offering a clear and concise look at why magnesium might be the missing element in your wellness routine.

Understanding the benefits of magnesium can transform how you approach your health. Imagine feeling more energized throughout the day and experiencing fewer headaches. Magnesium works at a cellular level to help your body function more efficiently, and its impact can be truly transformative. It supports over 300 biochemical reactions in the body and contributes to vital processes such as energy production and protein synthesis.

Whether you're an athlete seeking improved performance or someone simply looking to enhance daily health, magnesium holds the potential to make a significant difference. So, what should you do next? Discover the different forms of magnesium available and learn how to incorporate them into your diet or supplement regimen.

In this guide, we will talk about the following;

- What is Magnesium?
- How Does It Work?
- Understanding Magnesium Deficiency
- Use Cases of Magnesium
- Pros and Cons
- 5-Step Plan to Get Started with Magnesium
- Dietary Sources of Magnesium
- Sample Magnesium-Rich Recipes

Keep reading to learn more about the incredible benefits of magnesium and how you can start incorporating it into your daily routine. From better sleep to improved heart health, magnesium has the potential to impact every aspect of your well-being positively. By the end of this guide, you'll have a comprehensive understanding of how magnesium can support your health and the steps you can take to make it a part of your daily life.

CHAPTER 1
What is Magnesium?

Magnesium is a crucial mineral that plays a significant role in various bodily functions. It is the fourth most abundant mineral in the body and is responsible for over 300 biochemical reactions. Our bodies rely on magnesium to carry out vital processes such as energy production, muscle contraction, and DNA synthesis.

1. How Does Magnesium Work in Our Body?

Magnesium works in the body by acting as a cofactor in over 300 enzymatic reactions, which are crucial for various physiological functions. Here's how it contributes:

2. Energy Production

Magnesium is a critical component in the body's energy production processes, primarily through its role in forming ATP (adenosine triphosphate), the energy currency of the cell. ATP provides the energy required for many cellular functions, and magnesium is essential for stabilizing ATP molecules.

It acts as a co-factor in the conversion of nutrients from food into usable energy within the mitochondria, the powerhouse of the cell. Without sufficient magnesium, the efficiency of ATP production decreases, leading to potential fatigue and reduced energy levels.

3. Protein Synthesis

Magnesium plays a crucial role in synthesizing proteins, which are vital for cell growth, repair, and maintenance. It assists in the translation process, where amino acids are assembled into proteins based on the instructions encoded in mRNA.

Magnesium is a co-factor for the enzymes that facilitate this process, ensuring proteins are synthesized accurately and efficiently. Inadequate magnesium levels can impair protein synthesis, affecting muscle repair and growth, immune function, and the production of enzymes and hormones.

4. Muscle and Nerve Function

Magnesium is essential for proper muscle and nerve function because it helps regulate muscle contractions and nerve signals. It acts as a natural calcium blocker, balancing calcium levels in the body. When muscles contract, calcium enters the muscle cells, and magnesium helps them relax by counteracting calcium's effect.

This balance prevents conditions like muscle cramps and spasms. Additionally, magnesium is involved in transmitting nerve impulses, which are crucial for muscle coordination and overall nervous system function.

5. Blood Sugar Control

Magnesium is vital for regulating blood glucose levels, playing a role in insulin secretion and function. It enhances insulin sensitivity, allowing cells to effectively take in glucose from the bloodstream, which is crucial for maintaining energy balance.

Proper magnesium levels help prevent insulin resistance, a condition that can lead to type 2 diabetes. A deficiency in magnesium can disrupt glucose metabolism, contributing to elevated blood sugar levels and increased risk of diabetes.

6. Blood Pressure Regulation

Magnesium contributes to maintaining normal blood pressure by relaxing blood vessels and supporting cardiovascular health. It acts as a vasodilator, helping to widen blood vessels and improve blood flow, reducing the strain on the heart.

This mineral also aids in balancing electrolytes, such as sodium and potassium, which are essential for healthy blood pressure levels. Insufficient magnesium levels can result in high blood pressure, raising the likelihood of heart disease and stroke.

7. Bone Health

Magnesium is a key player in bone health, contributing to bone structure and the metabolism of calcium and vitamin D. It aids in the conversion of vitamin D to its active form, essential for the absorption of calcium. Magnesium also supports the structural integrity of bones by interacting with osteoblasts, the cells responsible for bone formation.

A deficiency in magnesium can lead to decreased bone density and strength, increasing the risk of osteoporosis and fractures. Maintaining adequate magnesium levels is crucial for preserving bone health and reducing the likelihood of bone-related disorders.

Overall, magnesium is vital for maintaining the body's biochemical balance and supporting overall health.

Health Benefits

Magnesium offers a variety of health benefits that are crucial for maintaining overall well-being:

1. Heart Health

Magnesium is crucial for maintaining cardiovascular health by regulating blood pressure and ensuring a stable heart rhythm. It acts as a natural calcium blocker, which helps relax blood vessels and improve blood flow, reducing the workload on the heart. This mineral's anti-inflammatory properties also help minimize arterial inflammation, lowering the risk of atherosclerosis.

Regular magnesium intake is associated with a reduced risk of heart disease, as it helps prevent hypertension and arrhythmias. A deficiency in magnesium can lead to increased blood pressure and a higher likelihood of cardiovascular events.

2. Mental Health

Magnesium plays a significant role in enhancing mood and alleviating symptoms of anxiety and depression. It supports the production of neurotransmitters like serotonin, which regulate mood and stress levels. By influencing the hypothalamic-pituitary-adrenal (HPA) axis, magnesium helps modulate the body's response to stress, promoting a sense of calm and well-being.

Low levels of magnesium can exacerbate mood disorders and increase susceptibility to anxiety and depression. Ensuring adequate magnesium intake contributes to better mental health by supporting the brain's biochemical balance.

3. Metabolic Processes

Magnesium is involved in numerous metabolic processes, particularly in regulating blood sugar levels. It enhances insulin sensitivity, allowing cells to efficiently absorb glucose from the bloodstream. This function is vital in preventing insulin resistance, which is a precursor to type 2 diabetes.

Magnesium also plays a role in carbohydrate metabolism, ensuring that energy is effectively produced from consumed food. A deficiency can disrupt these processes, increasing the risk of metabolic disorders and complicating the management of existing conditions.

4. Sleep Quality

Magnesium is known for its ability to promote relaxation and improve sleep quality. It regulates the production of melatonin, the hormone responsible for sleep-wake cycles, facilitating more restful and restorative sleep. By calming the nervous system and reducing stress, magnesium helps individuals fall asleep faster and enjoy deeper sleep stages.

Inadequate magnesium levels can lead to sleep disturbances and insomnia, affecting overall health and well-being. Consistent magnesium intake is essential for maintaining healthy sleep patterns and preventing sleep-related issues.

5. Chronic Disease Prevention

Regular magnesium intake is linked to a lower risk of developing chronic diseases such as type 2 diabetes, cardiovascular diseases, and migraines. Its anti-inflammatory properties help reduce chronic inflammation, a common factor in many long-term health issues. Magnesium's ability to regulate blood sugar, blood pressure, and lipid profiles contributes to its protective effects against chronic conditions.

A deficiency can increase the likelihood of these diseases, highlighting the importance of maintaining adequate magnesium levels for long-term health and disease prevention.

Overall, magnesium supports a wide range of bodily functions, contributing to enhanced physical and mental health, reducing the risk of chronic diseases, and promoting overall well-being.

Different Forms of Magnesium

Magnesium supplements come in various forms, each with unique properties and uses. Here's a rundown of some common forms:

1. Magnesium Citrate

Magnesium citrate is highly regarded for its excellent absorption rate, making it a popular choice for supplementation. This form of magnesium is particularly effective in supporting digestive health due to its mild laxative properties. It works by attracting water into the intestines, which can help improve bowel movements and relieve constipation.

This makes magnesium citrate a favorable option for individuals experiencing digestive discomfort or seeking to enhance gut motility. While generally well-tolerated, it can cause diarrhea if taken in excessive amounts, so proper dosing is important.

2. Magnesium Oxide

Magnesium oxide is known for its high magnesium concentration, though it has lower bioavailability compared to other forms. Despite this, it is commonly used to address short-term magnesium deficiencies due to its cost-effectiveness and availability. Additionally, magnesium oxide can be used as an antacid to alleviate digestive issues such as heartburn and indigestion.

However, its lower absorption rate means that larger doses may be necessary to achieve the desired effects, which can lead to gastrointestinal side effects like diarrhea or stomach upset in some individuals.

3. Magnesium Chloride

With good absorption properties, magnesium chloride is often used to maintain overall magnesium levels in the body. It is versatile and can be found in both oral supplements and topical applications. When applied topically, such as in bath salts and oils, magnesium chloride can aid in muscle relaxation and soothe sore muscles, making it a popular choice for athletes and individuals with muscle tension. While generally safe, topical use can sometimes cause skin irritation, especially in those with sensitive skin.

4. Magnesium Glycinate

Favored for its excellent absorption and gentle impact on the stomach, magnesium glycinate is widely used to promote relaxation and improve sleep quality. This variety of magnesium is linked to glycine, an amino acid with soothing properties, enhancing its ability to bolster mood and lessen anxiety symptoms.

Due to its gentle nature, magnesium glycinate is less likely to cause gastrointestinal distress, making it suitable for individuals with sensitive stomachs. It is a preferred option for those seeking to enhance mental well-being and improve sleep patterns.

5. Magnesium Sulfate

Magnesium sulfate, often referred to as Epsom salt, primarily utilized in baths, it helps relieve muscle soreness and reduce inflammation. Its efficacy in relaxing muscles and alleviating pain makes it a popular choice for post-exercise recovery and managing minor injuries.

While it can be ingested to relieve constipation due to its laxative properties, oral use is less common and should be done with caution to avoid potential side effects like dehydration and electrolyte imbalance. For most, topical application remains the safest and most effective use.

6. Magnesium Malate

Magnesium malate combines magnesium with malic acid, which is crucial for energy production in the body. This form is often recommended for individuals with chronic fatigue or fibromyalgia, as it may help reduce symptoms by supporting muscle function and enhancing ATP production.

The presence of malic acid, which is involved in the Krebs cycle, makes magnesium malate particularly beneficial for those seeking to boost energy levels and improve overall vitality. While generally well-tolerated, those with sensitivities to malic acid should consult with a healthcare provider before use.

Each type of magnesium supplement has specific benefits and is used to target different health needs. When choosing a supplement, it's important to consider the desired outcome, whether it's enhancing digestion, improving sleep, or supporting muscle health.

CHAPTER 2

Understanding Magnesium Deficiency

Magnesium deficiency, also known as hypomagnesemia, occurs when the body **does not have enough magnesium** to support essential physiological functions. Magnesium is a vital mineral involved in over 300 biochemical reactions in the body, including energy production, muscle and nerve function, and bone health.

Causes of Magnesium Deficiency

Magnesium deficiency can result from various factors, including lifestyle, dietary habits, and certain medical conditions. Here are some common causes:

1. **Inadequate Dietary Intake**: Consuming a diet low in magnesium-rich foods can lead to deficiency over time.
2. **Gastrointestinal Disorders**: Crohn's disease, celiac disease, and chronic diarrhea are examples of conditions that can interfere with magnesium absorption.
3. **Excessive Alcohol Consumption**: Alcohol can interfere with the body's ability to absorb and retain magnesium.
4. **Certain Medications**: Medications such as antibiotics, those for acid reflux, ulcers, and diuretics can impact magnesium levels in the body.

5. **Uncontrolled Diabetes**: Elevated blood sugar levels can cause the body to lose more magnesium through urine.
6. **Age**: Older adults are at higher risk due to decreased dietary intake and absorption efficiency.
7. **Stress**: Chronic stress can deplete magnesium levels in the body.
8. **Kidney Disease**: Impaired kidney function can result in increased excretion of magnesium.

Addressing these causes often involves dietary changes, lifestyle adjustments, and medical interventions as needed.

Symptoms of Magnesium Deficiency

Magnesium deficiency can lead to a variety of symptoms, some of which may be subtle at first. Here are common symptoms to watch for:

1. **Muscle Cramps and Spasms**: Muscle cramps, twitches, or spasms occurring frequently may indicate low magnesium levels.
2. **Fatigue and Weakness**: Feeling unusually tired or weak can be linked to magnesium deficiency.
3. **Nausea and Vomiting**: These digestive issues can occur with low magnesium.
4. **Loss of Appetite**: A decreased desire to eat might be related to insufficient magnesium.
5. **Numbness and Tingling**: Experiencing tingling or numbness, especially in the extremities, can be a symptom.
6. **Personality Changes**: Mood swings, anxiety, or depression may be associated with low magnesium.
7. **Abnormal Heart Rhythms**: An irregular heartbeat or palpitations can occur with magnesium deficiency.
8. **Osteoporosis**: Long-term deficiency can contribute to bone health issues.

If you suspect you have a magnesium deficiency, it's important to consult with a healthcare professional for proper diagnosis and treatment.

How to Diagnose Magnesium Deficiency

1. Diagnosing magnesium deficiency can be challenging, as blood tests only measure magnesium levels in the blood, which represent a small portion of the body's total magnesium content. Here's how healthcare providers typically approach diagnosis:
2. **Symptom Assessment**: Doctors will consider symptoms in conjunction with dietary and lifestyle factors to assess the likelihood of deficiency.
3. **Blood Tests**: Serum magnesium tests are commonly used, although they may not always reflect true magnesium status. More comprehensive tests like the RBC magnesium test can provide a better overview.
4. **24-Hour Urinary Excretion Test**: This test helps evaluate how much magnesium is being excreted, offering insights into whether the deficiency is due to poor intake or increased loss.
5. **Medical and Dietary History**: A detailed review of the patient's medical history, diet, and lifestyle can help identify potential causes of deficiency.
6. **Magnesium Loading Test**: In certain cases, a magnesium loading test may be conducted to assess the body's retention capacity, although this is less common.

Addressing magnesium deficiency involves dietary changes, supplementation, and managing underlying conditions. By understanding and recognizing the signs and causes of magnesium deficiency, individuals can take proactive steps to maintain optimal magnesium levels and support overall health.

Addressing Magnesium Deficiency

Addressing magnesium deficiency involves dietary changes and, if necessary, supplementation:

Supplementation

While dietary sources are preferable, supplements may be necessary for those unable to meet their magnesium needs through food alone. Here's what you need to know about magnesium supplementation:

- **When to Consider Supplements**: If you have a health condition that inhibits nutrient absorption, follow a restrictive diet, or have increased magnesium needs due to pregnancy or intense physical activity, supplements might be beneficial. However, it's crucial to establish this need through professional guidance.
- **Types of Magnesium Supplements**: Magnesium supplements come in various forms, including magnesium citrate, magnesium oxide, and magnesium glycinate. Each type has different absorption rates and uses. For example, magnesium citrate is often used to relieve constipation, while magnesium glycinate is more gentle on the stomach and can be better for long-term use.
- **Consulting a Healthcare Provider**: Before starting any supplement, consult a healthcare provider to determine the appropriate dosage and form, as excessive magnesium can lead to side effects like diarrhea, nausea, or abdominal cramping. A healthcare provider can help tailor supplementation to your individual health profile and needs.
- **Choosing the Right Supplement**: Look for high-quality brands that are verified by third-party testers to ensure purity

and potency. Opt for supplements that suit your dietary preferences, such as vegan or gluten-free options.

By understanding both dietary sources and supplementation, you can make informed decisions to maintain optimal magnesium levels, supporting your overall health and well-being.

Risk Factors and Susceptible Populations

Certain populations are more susceptible to magnesium deficiency, including:

- **Older Adults**: As people age, their dietary intake often decreases, and the body may become less efficient at absorbing essential nutrients. This dual challenge can significantly increase the risk of magnesium deficiency, which plays a crucial role in many bodily functions, including muscle and nerve function.
- **Individuals with Gastrointestinal Disorders**: Crohn's disease, celiac disease, and irritable bowel syndrome are conditions that can disrupt the body's efficient nutrient absorption. As a result, those with gastrointestinal disorders face a heightened risk of magnesium deficiency, which can exacerbate their overall health issues.
- **People with Type 2 Diabetes**: People with type 2 diabetes frequently face increased magnesium loss in urine because of elevated blood sugar levels. This depletion can result in a deficiency, making blood sugar management more challenging and potentially leading to further diabetes-related complications.

- **Alcoholics**: Consistent alcohol consumption can significantly disrupt the body's capacity to absorb and maintain magnesium. Alcohol hampers the intestinal absorption of nutrients and can also cause persistent inflammation, both of which severely diminish magnesium levels and lead to various health issues.

Correcting magnesium deficiency is essential for maintaining overall health and preventing complications like cardiovascular diseases, osteoporosis, and mental health disorders. Regular check-ups and a balanced diet can help manage and prevent magnesium deficiency effectively.

CHAPTER 3

Use Cases of Magnesium

Now that we have established the importance of magnesium in maintaining overall health, let's explore some specific use cases where it plays a vital role.

Muscle Cramps and Spasms

Magnesium is well-known for its ability to alleviate muscle cramps and spasms, a benefit particularly valued by athletes and those with magnesium deficiency. It functions as a natural muscle relaxant by counteracting calcium, which stimulates muscle contraction. By promoting relaxation, magnesium reduces both the frequency and intensity of muscle cramps.

This mineral helps stabilize neuromuscular junctions, preventing the excessive excitation that can lead to involuntary muscle contractions. Regular magnesium supplementation can be especially beneficial for individuals engaged in vigorous physical activities or those experiencing electrolyte imbalances.

Migraines

Regular magnesium supplementation has been shown to decrease the frequency and severity of migraine attacks. Magnesium stabilizes nerve cells by regulating neurotransmitter release and preventing excessive neuronal firing, which are common triggers for migraines.

It also helps reduce inflammation and vasoconstriction, both of which contribute to migraine pathophysiology. Individuals prone to migraines often have lower intracellular magnesium levels, and supplementation can help restore balance, offering a natural approach to migraine prevention and management.

Anxiety and Stress

Magnesium plays a critical role in modulating mood by regulating neurotransmitters such as serotonin, which influences anxiety and stress levels. It acts on the hypothalamic-pituitary-adrenal (HPA) axis to reduce the body's stress response, promoting relaxation and mental well-being.

Low magnesium levels are associated with heightened anxiety and stress, making supplementation a viable option for alleviating these symptoms. By supporting the biochemical pathways that manage mood, magnesium contributes to emotional stability and a calmer state of mind.

Insomnia

Known for its calming effects, magnesium is often used to improve sleep quality. It aids in the regulation of melatonin, the hormone responsible for sleep-wake cycles, facilitating restful and uninterrupted sleep.

Magnesium's ability to calm the nervous system also helps individuals fall asleep more easily and enjoy deeper sleep stages. For those struggling with insomnia, magnesium supplementation can be a natural solution to enhance sleep quality and promote a more restorative sleep experience.

Athletic Performance and Recovery

Athletes frequently use magnesium to boost performance and support muscle recovery. It plays a crucial role in energy production by aiding in ATP synthesis, which fuels muscular activity. Magnesium also reduces oxidative stress and inflammation, accelerating recovery post-exercise.

By preventing muscle cramps and supporting efficient energy utilization, magnesium helps athletes maintain peak performance and recover effectively from intense physical activities.

Cardiovascular Health

Magnesium is vital for cardiovascular health, contributing to the regulation of blood pressure and maintenance of a steady heart rhythm. It acts as a natural calcium channel blocker, relaxing blood vessels and improving circulation, which reduces the risk of hypertension.

Additionally, magnesium's anti-inflammatory properties protect against atherosclerosis, lowering the likelihood of heart disease. Regular magnesium intake supports heart function and is associated with a reduced risk of cardiovascular events.

Bone Health

Essential for bone formation, magnesium plays a significant role in maintaining bone density and strength. It is involved in the metabolism of calcium and vitamin D, both critical for healthy bones.

Magnesium deficiency can lead to weakened bones and an increased risk of osteoporosis. Supplementation or a diet rich in magnesium can help prevent bone demineralization and support skeletal health.

Digestive Health

Magnesium is effective in relieving constipation thanks to its laxative properties. It draws water into the intestines, softening stool and promoting bowel movements. Magnesium citrate, in particular, is commonly used to improve digestive health, providing relief from constipation. Adequate magnesium intake ensures regularity and supports overall gastrointestinal function.

Metabolic Health

Magnesium supports metabolic processes by enhancing insulin sensitivity and regulating blood sugar levels. It plays a crucial role in carbohydrate metabolism and energy production, contributing to the prevention and management of metabolic conditions such as type 2 diabetes.

Magnesium deficiency is linked to impaired glucose control and increased risk of insulin resistance, underscoring the importance of maintaining adequate magnesium levels for optimal metabolic health.

Overall, magnesium is integral to various health applications, supporting physical and mental health while contributing to the prevention and management of numerous conditions.

CHAPTER 4
Pros and Cons

Magnesium is a vital mineral renowned for its essential role in maintaining health and wellness. Widely used in supplements and found in various dietary sources, magnesium supports numerous bodily functions, from muscle health to energy production.

While it offers significant advantages, such as enhancing mood and promoting cardiovascular health, it's crucial to also consider potential drawbacks like digestive discomfort and medication interactions. Understanding both the pros and cons of magnesium allows for informed decisions in integrating this beneficial mineral into your health regimen.

Pros

Magnesium is an incredibly advantageous mineral that plays a crucial role in enhancing daily life. Here are some key advantages of incorporating magnesium into your routine:

1. Affordability

Magnesium supplements and magnesium-rich foods are generally affordable, making it accessible for most people to include in their diet without straining their budget. Many options, such as leafy greens, nuts, seeds, and whole grains, are not only cost-effective but also widely available in grocery stores and markets. This affordability allows individuals to easily incorporate magnesium into their daily meals, promoting overall health without financial stress.

2. Variety of Forms

Magnesium is available in numerous forms, including tablets, powders, capsules, and even topical applications like creams and sprays. This wide range of options allows individuals to easily tailor their magnesium intake to suit their personal preferences and specific health needs.

Whether someone prefers the convenience of a tablet, the versatility of a powder that can be mixed into drinks, or the targeted relief offered by topical applications, there is a suitable magnesium option for everyone. This adaptability makes it easier for people to incorporate magnesium into their daily routines, ultimately supporting their overall health and wellness.

3. Ease of Supplementation

Incorporating magnesium into your diet is straightforward and accessible, whether through supplements or abundant natural food sources. Foods rich in magnesium, such as nuts, seeds, whole grains, and leafy greens, not only provide this essential mineral but also come with a host of additional nutrients and health benefits.

This simplicity in sourcing magnesium makes it easy to maintain optimal levels in the body, ensuring you can support vital functions such as muscle and nerve function, blood sugar control, and bone health with minimal effort in your daily nutrition.

4. Supports a Balanced Diet

Magnesium plays a crucial role in contributing to a well-rounded diet by supporting numerous bodily functions. It aids in muscle health by enabling proper muscle contraction and relaxation, which is vital for both athletic performance and everyday activities.

Additionally, magnesium is essential for energy production, as it helps convert food into usable energy, allowing us to stay active and alert throughout the day. By ensuring adequate magnesium intake, we can enhance our overall health and vitality, promoting better physical performance and improving our quality of life.

5. Minimal Side Effects

When used appropriately, magnesium is known for its minimal side effects, which makes it a safe and beneficial addition to most health regimens. Unlike many medications or supplements that can lead to adverse reactions, magnesium is gentle on the body. This gentle nature allows individuals to incorporate it into their daily routines without significant risk of negative impacts.

Moreover, magnesium not only supports various bodily functions, such as muscle and nerve function, but it also contributes to overall well-being by helping to regulate mood and promote restful sleep. As a result, it can be an ideal choice for those seeking to improve their health naturally and sustainably.

6. Enhances Lifestyle and Wellness

Magnesium is essential for supporting several key bodily functions that contribute to overall health and wellness. It aids in muscle relaxation, which helps to prevent cramps and promotes recovery after physical activity.

Additionally, magnesium has a calming effect on the nervous system, effectively reducing stress and anxiety levels. This mineral is also linked to improved sleep quality, as it helps regulate neurotransmitters that send signals to the brain to prepare for rest. By incorporating adequate magnesium into your diet, you can significantly enhance your lifestyle and promote a deeper sense of well-being, leading to a more balanced and fulfilling life.

Overall, magnesium's practical advantages make it an essential component of a healthy lifestyle, offering simple and effective ways to boost wellness and support various health needs.

Cons

While magnesium offers numerous health benefits, there are a few disadvantages to consider, though they are generally outweighed by the advantages:

1. **Digestive Discomfort**: High doses of magnesium, especially from supplements, can sometimes lead to digestive issues such as diarrhea or stomach upset. However, these effects are typically mild and can often be alleviated by adjusting the dosage or switching the form of magnesium.
2. **Medication Interactions**: Magnesium can interact with certain medications, such as some antibiotics or drugs for osteoporosis, potentially affecting their absorption or efficacy. It's important to consult with a healthcare provider to manage these interactions effectively.

3. **Need for Proper Dosage**: Ensuring the correct dosage is crucial to avoid side effects and maximize benefits. Overconsumption can lead to an imbalance or toxicity, although this is rare and usually only occurs with excessive supplementation.

Despite these potential drawbacks, magnesium remains a valuable nutrient due to its wide-ranging benefits. It supports muscle function, enhances mood, improves sleep quality, and contributes to cardiovascular and bone health. When used appropriately, the advantages of magnesium far surpass the minor disadvantages, making it an essential mineral for overall well-being.

Potential Side Effects

Magnesium provides numerous health benefits, but it can also present some unique side effects if not taken appropriately. Here are a few potential side effects to watch out for:

1. **Magnesium Toxicity**: Although rare, consuming very high doses of magnesium, especially through supplements, can lead to toxicity. Symptoms may include nausea, vomiting, low blood pressure, confusion, slowed breathing, and irregular heartbeat. It's critical to adhere to recommended dosages to prevent this condition.
2. **Interactions with Medications**: Magnesium can affect the absorption and effectiveness of certain medications, including some antibiotics and osteoporosis treatments. This interaction may reduce the efficacy of these medications, so it's important to consult with healthcare providers to manage these potential conflicts.

3. **Impaired Kidney Function**: Individuals with compromised kidney function should exercise caution when taking magnesium, as their bodies may struggle to eliminate excess magnesium, increasing the risk of side effects.
4. **Neurological Effects**: In rare cases, excessive magnesium intake can lead to neurological symptoms, such as lethargy or confusion, especially in individuals with underlying health issues.

To safely enjoy the benefits of magnesium, it's essential to follow recommended dosages and seek advice from healthcare professionals, particularly if you're taking other medications or have existing health conditions.

CHAPTER 5

5-Step Plan to Get Started with Magnesium

Incorporating magnesium into your daily routine can seem daunting, but it doesn't have to be. Here's a simple 5-step plan to help you get started:

Step 1: Consult Your Healthcare Provider

Embarking on your magnesium supplementation journey should begin with a thorough consultation with your healthcare provider. This initial step is crucial for ensuring that your approach to magnesium is both safe and suitable for your individual health needs. Here's why this step is so important:

Personalized Medical Advice

Your healthcare provider can offer personalized medical advice tailored to your unique health profile. They have a comprehensive understanding of your medical history, current medications, and any pre-existing conditions, all of which are essential factors in determining whether magnesium supplementation is appropriate for you.

By discussing your health goals and concerns, your provider can help you understand how magnesium might fit into your overall health strategy.

Understanding Potential Health Benefits

Magnesium is known for offering a variety of health benefits, including supporting muscle and nerve function, promoting bone health, and aiding in energy production. It may also play a role in managing conditions such as hypertension, migraines, and certain types of heart disease.

Your healthcare provider can help you explore these potential benefits and determine which are most relevant to your health needs, ensuring that your supplementation plan is aligned with your wellness objectives.

Assessing Potential Risks

While magnesium is generally safe for most people, it's important to be aware of potential risks, especially if you have specific health conditions or are taking certain medications. Excessive magnesium intake can lead to adverse effects such as gastrointestinal upset or more serious complications. Consulting with your healthcare provider allows you to assess these risks and make informed decisions about the appropriate dosage and form of magnesium for your situation.

Tailored Supplementation Plan

Based on the insights gained from your consultation, your healthcare provider can help design a supplementation plan that is tailored to your individual health needs. This plan will consider factors such as your age, dietary intake, lifestyle, and specific health goals.

By following a customized plan, you can maximize the benefits of magnesium supplementation while minimizing potential risks, ensuring a balanced and effective approach to your health management.

By prioritizing a healthcare provider's guidance, you lay a solid foundation for a successful and beneficial magnesium supplementation journey.

Step 2: Choose the Right Form of Magnesium

Selecting the appropriate form of magnesium is a key step in optimizing your supplementation strategy. With a variety of magnesium forms available, understanding their unique benefits and applications is essential. Here's a detailed look at how to choose the right form of magnesium based on your health goals:

Understanding Different Forms of Magnesium

Magnesium supplements come in several forms, each with its own absorption rate and health benefits:

- **Magnesium Citrate**: Known for its high absorption rate, magnesium citrate is often recommended for those who need to increase magnesium levels quickly. It's also beneficial for managing constipation due to its gentle laxative effect.
- **Magnesium Oxide**: Often used to address digestive issues, magnesium oxide is less readily absorbed than other forms but can be effective for alleviating symptoms like heartburn and indigestion.
- **Magnesium Glycinate**: This form is known for its calming properties and is often used to support sleep and reduce

anxiety. It is gentle on the stomach and less likely to cause digestive upset.
- **Magnesium Malate**: Known for its energy-boosting properties, magnesium malate is often recommended for individuals with fatigue or fibromyalgia due to its role in energy production.
- **Magnesium Threonate**: This form has been studied for its ability to cross the blood-brain barrier, potentially offering cognitive benefits and supporting brain health.

Aligning with Health Goals

Choosing the right form of magnesium should align with your specific health objectives. For example, if you are looking to improve sleep quality, magnesium glycinate might be the best option. If digestive health is a concern, magnesium oxide could be more suitable. Understanding your health goals can help you select the form that provides the most benefits for your needs.

Guidance from Healthcare Providers and Pharmacists

Your healthcare provider and pharmacist are invaluable resources in the selection process. They can provide insights based on your medical history, current health status, and any medications you are taking. Their expertise ensures you choose a form of magnesium that complements your overall health plan, minimizes potential interactions, and maximizes effectiveness.

Tailored Supplementation Plan

By consulting with healthcare professionals, you can develop a supplementation plan that is tailored to your unique health profile. This personalized approach ensures that you are using the right form of magnesium to achieve your health goals safely and effectively.

By carefully selecting the form of magnesium that best suits your individual needs, you can enhance your overall health strategy and achieve optimal benefits from your supplementation.

Step 3: Determine the Correct Dosage

After selecting the appropriate form of magnesium, the next crucial step is to determine the correct dosage. This decision is vital to ensure that you reap the benefits of magnesium without encountering any adverse effects. Here's a guide to understanding the factors influencing magnesium dosage and the importance of professional guidance:

Factors Influencing Magnesium Dosage

The appropriate dosage of magnesium can vary significantly from person to person, influenced by several factors:

- **Age**: Magnesium needs can change with age. For instance, children require lower doses compared to adults, while older adults might need adjustments due to changes in metabolism and dietary absorption.
- **Sex**: Men and women have different nutritional needs, including magnesium. Women may have varying magnesium requirements based on hormonal changes, pregnancy, or lactation.
- **Health Conditions**: Specific health issues may necessitate adjustments in magnesium dosage. Conditions such as kidney disease, gastrointestinal disorders, or diabetes can affect how your body processes magnesium, necessitating a tailored dosage plan.
-

- **Lifestyle Factors**: Dietary habits, physical activity levels, and stress can all impact magnesium needs. A healthcare provider can help assess how these factors influence your optimal dosage.

Importance of Healthcare Provider Recommendations

Consulting with your healthcare provider to determine the correct dosage is essential. They can evaluate your personal health profile and provide a dosage recommendation that considers all relevant factors. Their expertise helps ensure that you use magnesium safely and effectively, minimizing the risk of interactions with medications or exacerbating existing health conditions.

Potential Side Effects of Incorrect Dosages

Taking magnesium inappropriately can lead to undesirable side effects. Excessive magnesium intake may cause symptoms like diarrhea, nausea, or abdominal cramping. In severe cases, it can lead to more serious complications, such as irregular heartbeats or low blood pressure. Conversely, inadequate magnesium levels might not provide the desired health benefits, leaving conditions unaddressed.

Adhering to the Recommended Dosage

Following the dosage recommended by your healthcare provider is critical. It ensures that you receive the right amount of magnesium to support your health goals while minimizing potential risks. Regular follow-ups with your provider can help adjust the dosage as needed, responding to changes in your health status or lifestyle.

By carefully determining and adhering to the correct magnesium dosage, you can effectively integrate this essential mineral into your health regimen, maximizing its benefits and maintaining your well-being.

Step 4: Incorporate Magnesium into Your Daily Routine

Establishing a consistent routine for taking your magnesium supplement is key to maximizing its benefits and ensuring steady absorption. Here's how to smoothly integrate magnesium into your everyday life:

The Benefits of Consistency

Taking magnesium at the same time each day is beneficial for maintaining a stable level of this essential mineral in your body. This consistency is crucial because it can significantly enhance magnesium's effectiveness in supporting your overall health goals, such as improved muscle function, better sleep quality, and increased energy levels.

By establishing a regular intake routine, your body has the opportunity to adapt to the supplement, which minimizes potential side effects like digestive discomfort and optimizes the health benefits over time.

Moreover, consistency in supplement intake helps in building a lasting habit, making it easier to remember to take your magnesium daily. Setting a specific time, such as alongside a meal or before bed, can serve as a helpful reminder.

Additionally, you might consider using a pill organizer or setting a daily alarm on your phone to further reinforce this habit. Over time, these practices can contribute to your overall well-being and ensure that you are reaping the full benefits of magnesium supplementation.

Tips for Remembering Your Supplement

Creating a routine around your magnesium intake can aid in making it a seamless part of your day:

- **Set a Daily Reminder**: Consider using a phone alarm or calendar notification to remind you to take your magnesium at the same time each day. This consistent timing not only helps establish a routine but also ensures that you don't forget to take your supplement amidst your daily activities.
- **Integrate with Existing Routines**: Try to link your magnesium intake to a daily habit you already have, such as brushing your teeth or enjoying your morning breakfast. By associating it with a familiar activity, you create a natural trigger that can enhance your memory and make it easier to remember to take your magnesium regularly.
- **Use a Pill Organizer**: A weekly pill organizer can be incredibly helpful for managing your supplements. By pre-sorting your magnesium and any other vitamins you take, you can visually confirm each dose is taken, ensuring you never miss a day. This method also simplifies your routine, allowing you to stay organized and focused on your health goals.

Deciding When to Take Magnesium

The timing of your magnesium intake can influence its effectiveness:

With a Meal

Taking magnesium alongside food can significantly enhance its absorption in the body while also minimizing the likelihood of gastrointestinal discomfort. This method is particularly beneficial for individuals with sensitive stomachs or those prone to digestive issues, as the presence of food can buffer the magnesium and facilitate smoother digestion.

Additionally, consuming magnesium with meals can help ensure that it is more readily utilized by the body, making it an excellent choice for anyone looking to optimize their mineral intake while avoiding potential stomach upset.

On an Empty Stomach

Conversely, some forms of magnesium, such as magnesium citrate, may be better absorbed when taken on an empty stomach, as there are fewer competing substances in the digestive tract. This method can lead to more efficient uptake of the mineral, but it may not be suitable for everyone.

Therefore, it's crucial to consult with your healthcare provider to determine if this approach aligns with your individual health needs and lifestyle. They can guide you on the best timing for magnesium supplementation to maximize its benefits while considering your overall digestive health.

Personalizing Your Routine

Discuss with your healthcare provider to tailor your magnesium routine to your specific needs. They can advise you on the best time of day to take magnesium based on your lifestyle and dietary habits, ensuring you receive the maximum benefit without compromising comfort.

By integrating magnesium into your daily routine, you establish a foundation for consistent supplementation, paving the way for improved health and wellness outcomes.

Step 5: Monitoring the Effects of Magnesium Supplementation

As you embark on your magnesium supplementation journey, it's essential to closely observe how your body responds to this new addition to your health regimen. Monitoring its effects helps you gauge its benefits and address any potential issues promptly. Here's a detailed guide on how to effectively track and respond to the changes you experience:

What Changes to Look For

Magnesium can influence various aspects of your health, and being mindful of specific changes can help you assess its impact:

- **Energy Levels**: Take note of any noticeable changes in your daily energy and fatigue levels throughout the day. Magnesium plays a crucial role in energy production at a cellular level, so incorporating it into your routine might lead to increased vitality and improved stamina during physical activities.
- **Sleep Quality**: Pay attention to any enhancements in your sleep patterns, such as falling asleep more easily or experiencing deeper sleep. Magnesium is well-known for its calming properties, which can help relax the nervous system, thereby improving sleep quality and duration, and making you feel more refreshed upon waking.
- **Muscle Function**: Observe any differences in muscle cramps, tension, or overall muscle function during your workouts or daily activities. Magnesium supports muscle relaxation by assisting in the regulation of muscle contractions, potentially aiding in reducing cramps and enhancing overall muscle performance.
- **Mood and Stress Levels**: Since magnesium can have a calming effect on the mind and body, track any changes

in your mood or stress levels over time. You might notice improvements in anxiety, irritability, or overall feelings of well-being, as magnesium has been linked to better emotional regulation and stress management.

How to Track Changes Effectively

Keeping a detailed record of your experiences can provide valuable insights into how magnesium is affecting your health:

1. Journal Your Observations

Take the time each day to write down detailed notes on any noticeable changes in your energy levels, sleep quality, mood fluctuations, and any physical symptoms you may experience. By consistently documenting these observations, you can track trends over weeks or months.

This practice can reveal patterns that highlight the positive or negative effects of your supplementation, helping you make informed decisions about your health.

2. Use Health Apps

Consider leveraging mobile applications specifically designed to monitor various health metrics, such as sleep patterns, mood tracking, and dietary habits. These digital tools not only allow you to systematically track your changes but also provide visual representations of your data over time.

Many of these apps even offer features to share your progress with healthcare providers, making it easier to have informed discussions about your health journey.

3. Regular Self-Assessments

Make it a priority to schedule regular self-assessments to evaluate key health indicators, such as weight, energy levels, and overall well-being. This structured approach will help you stay attuned to any significant shifts in your health status.

By reviewing these assessments periodically, you can identify trends and make proactive adjustments to your routine or supplementation, ensuring that you remain aligned with your health goals.

Communicating with Your Healthcare Provider

If you experience any adverse effects or have concerns, it's crucial to consult your healthcare provider:

4. Report Any Adverse Effects

It is crucial to communicate any symptoms you experience, such as gastrointestinal discomfort, headaches, or other unusual changes, with your healthcare provider. Open dialogue about these issues not only helps in identifying the underlying causes but also allows for the adjustment of your supplementation plan if necessary, ensuring that it aligns with your overall health goals.

5. Reassess Your Plan

Engaging in regular check-ins with your healthcare provider is essential for maintaining optimal health. These appointments provide an opportunity for timely reassessment of your magnesium dosage or form, which is vital for adapting to any changes in your body's needs or lifestyle.

By consistently reviewing your plan, you can ensure that your magnesium supplementation remains effective and relevant to your health status.

6. Collaborative Approach

Adopting a collaborative approach is key to achieving the best health outcomes. By working closely with your healthcare provider, you can fine-tune your supplementation strategy based on their expertise and insights. This partnership not only empowers you to make informed decisions about your health but also ensures that your magnesium intake is optimized for your unique circumstances and health objectives.

By diligently monitoring the effects of magnesium and maintaining open communication with your healthcare provider, you can ensure that your supplementation journey is both safe and beneficial, leading to improved overall well-being.

By following this step-by-step approach, you can effectively integrate magnesium into your lifestyle and enjoy its numerous health benefits, including improved muscle function, enhanced sleep quality, and better overall wellness.

Tips for Increasing Magnesium Intake

Dietary Tips and Meal Planning

Incorporating magnesium-rich foods into your daily diet can significantly boost your intake of this essential mineral. Here are some practical tips and meal-planning ideas:

1. Breakfast Boost

Start your day off right with a nutrient-packed smoothie that energizes your morning. Blend together a generous handful of fresh spinach, a ripe banana for natural sweetness, a cup of almond milk for creaminess, and a tablespoon of chia seeds for added fiber and omega-3s.

This delightful combination not only provides a solid magnesium foundation to kickstart your day but is also quick and easy to prepare, making it perfect for busy mornings.

2. Nutty Snacks

Keep a stash of mixed nuts, such as almonds and cashews, within reach for a convenient and healthy snacking option that is perfect for any time of day. These nutritious nuts are not only portable and easy to store, but they are also rich in magnesium, a vital mineral that plays a crucial role in maintaining overall well-being, supporting everything from muscle function to heart health.

You can enjoy them on their own as a quick snack to curb hunger or get creative by sprinkling them over creamy yogurt or warm oatmeal. This not only adds an extra crunch but also enhances the flavor and texture of your meals. Plus, the added nutrients from the nuts will provide a sustained energy boost throughout the day, helping you stay alert and focused, whether you're working, exercising, or just going about your daily activities.

3. Leafy Green Salads

Make salads a staple in your meals to increase your intake of magnesium-rich foods. Use a variety of leafy greens such as spinach, kale, and Swiss chard, which are not only packed with nutrients but also add vibrant colors to your plate.

Enhance the flavor and nutritional profile by adding creamy avocado, crunchy pumpkin seeds, and a drizzle of high-quality olive oil. This combination creates a delicious and nutritious option that can be enjoyed for lunch or dinner.

4. Recipe Ideas

Consider whipping up dishes like a refreshing quinoa salad loaded with black beans, corn, and diced bell peppers for a colorful and magnesium-rich meal. Alternatively, try making a spinach and mushroom frittata, which is packed with veggies and perfect for breakfast or brunch.

Both recipes are rich in magnesium and can be easily prepared in advance, making them ideal for meal prepping and quick weeknight dinners.

Lifestyle Changes to Enhance Magnesium Absorption

Beyond diet, certain lifestyle habits can enhance how effectively your body absorbs magnesium:

1. Limit Caffeine and Alcohol

Both caffeine and alcohol can significantly interfere with the body's ability to absorb magnesium, which is vital for numerous bodily functions. It's advisable to monitor and reduce your intake of these beverages, particularly if you find yourself consuming them in large quantities or on a regular basis. Consider substituting with herbal teas or sparkling water to help decrease your dependence on caffeinated and alcoholic drinks.

2. Manage Stress

Chronic stress can have a profound negative impact on magnesium levels in the body, leading to a range of health issues. To counter this, it's essential to incorporate effective stress-reducing practices into your daily routine.

Activities such as meditation, yoga, or even simple deep breathing exercises can help calm the mind and body, promoting not only better magnesium levels but also overall well-being.

3. Get Enough Vitamin D

Vitamin D is crucial for the body's ability to absorb magnesium efficiently. To ensure you're getting enough vitamin D, make it a habit to spend time outdoors in sunlight, especially during the warmer months.

If sunlight exposure is limited, such as during winter, consider taking a vitamin D supplement after consulting with a healthcare provider to maintain optimal levels and support magnesium absorption.

4. Stay Hydrated

Maintaining adequate hydration is essential for overall health and well-being. Drinking enough water not only supports various bodily functions but also aids in the digestive process, which is key for improving mineral absorption, including magnesium.

Aim to drink at least 8 glasses of water a day, and consider increasing your intake during hot weather or physical activity to ensure your body stays properly hydrated.

By making these dietary adjustments and lifestyle changes, you can effectively increase your magnesium intake and enhance your overall well-being. Consider these tips as part of a holistic approach to maintaining optimal health and vitality.

CHAPTER 6

Dietary Sources of Magnesium

Magnesium is an essential mineral that plays a critical role in numerous bodily functions. Ensuring an adequate intake of magnesium through your diet can help maintain optimal health. This section explores some of the best dietary sources of magnesium, tips on how to prepare these foods to retain their magnesium content, and considerations for specific dietary preferences.

Magnesium-Rich Foods

Magnesium-rich foods are essential for maintaining good health, as magnesium plays a crucial role in many bodily functions. Here are some foods that are high in magnesium:

1. **Leafy Greens**: Kale, Swiss chard, and spinach are excellent sources.
2. **Nuts and Seeds**: Almonds, cashews, and pumpkin seeds are particularly high in magnesium.
3. **Whole Grains**: Quinoa, whole wheat bread, and brown rice offer a substantial amount of magnesium.
4. **Legumes**: Lentils, chickpeas, and black beans are high in magnesium.

5. **Fish**: Fatty fish like salmon and mackerel contain magnesium.
6. **Avocados**: This versatile fruit is not only rich in healthy fats but also magnesium.
7. **Dark Chocolate**: A delicious source of magnesium, but best consumed in moderation.
8. **Bananas**: Known for their potassium, bananas also offer magnesium.

Including these foods in your diet can help you meet your daily magnesium needs.

Cooking and Preparation Tips

To maximize magnesium intake from foods, consider the following tips:

1. Minimize Cooking Time

Overcooking vegetables can lead to significant nutrient loss, particularly when it comes to essential vitamins and minerals. To preserve their nutritional value, consider steaming vegetables like spinach and Swiss chard. This gentle cooking method, often referred to as steaming or poaching, helps retain the magnesium content found in various ingredients, such as leafy greens and nuts.

By utilizing this technique, you're not only preserving important nutrients but also ensuring that you get the maximum health benefits associated with magnesium, which plays a vital role in numerous bodily functions. Plus, this method allows you to enjoy the vibrant flavors and natural textures of the food, making your meals both nutritious and delicious.

2. Soak Nuts and Seeds

Although nuts and seeds are excellent sources of magnesium, providing substantial amounts of this essential mineral, they also contain phytic acid. Phytic acid can bind to minerals, potentially inhibiting their absorption in the body. This means that while you may be consuming these nutritious foods, your body might not be able to fully benefit from the nutrients they offer.

To effectively reduce the phytic acid content in nuts and seeds, a simple yet effective method is soaking them in water for several hours before consumption. This process not only helps break down phytic acid but also reduces the levels of other antinutrients present.

Soaking activates enzymes that aid in the digestion process, making it easier for your body to absorb essential vitamins and minerals such as magnesium, iron, and zinc. By taking this extra step, you can enhance the nutritional profile of your snacks and meals, ensuring that you get the maximum benefit from these healthy foods.

3. Choose Whole Grains

Opting for whole grains over refined versions is a smart choice for anyone looking to boost their magnesium intake. Whole grains, such as brown rice, quinoa, and whole wheat, retain the mineral-rich outer layers that are often stripped away during processing.

By incorporating these nutrient-dense grains into your diet, you not only increase your magnesium intake but also benefit from the additional fiber and nutrients that support overall health.

Cooking methods can significantly impact magnesium content. For instance, boiling can cause magnesium to leach into the water, so steaming or sautéing is preferable. Additionally, raw consumption of nuts and seeds preserves their magnesium content, as roasting can reduce it.

Considerations for Different Diets

Vegan and Vegetarian Diets

- **Legumes**: Beans and lentils, such as black beans and chickpeas, are rich in magnesium and protein, making them staples in plant-based diets.
- **Tofu and Tempeh**: These soy-based products provide significant amounts of magnesium and can be easily incorporated into various dishes.

Gluten-Free Diets

- **Buckwheat and Millet**: Both are excellent gluten-free grains rich in magnesium and can be used in place of wheat-based grains.
- **Amaranth**: Another gluten-free grain, amaranth offers a significant magnesium boost and can be used in porridge or baking.

Keto Diets

- **Avocados**: A keto-friendly food, avocados are rich in magnesium and healthy fats, making them ideal for those on low-carb diets.
- **Dark Chocolate**: In moderation, dark chocolate (at least 70% cocoa) is an excellent source of magnesium and fits well within keto guidelines.

By incorporating a variety of magnesium-rich foods and considering your dietary preferences, you can ensure an adequate intake of this essential mineral. Whether you're adjusting your cooking methods or selecting specific foods, these strategies can help you maintain sufficient magnesium levels for optimal health.

CHAPTER 7

Sample Magnesium-Rich Recipes

In this chapter, we will provide some delicious and easy-to-make recipes that are rich in magnesium. Incorporating these recipes into your regular meal plan can help boost your magnesium intake.

Spinach and Banana Smoothie Bowl

Ingredients:

- 1 cup fresh spinach leaves
- 1 ripe banana
- 1 cup almond milk
- 2 tablespoons chia seeds
- 1/4 cup sliced almonds
- 1/4 cup mixed berries (optional)

Instructions:

1. In a blender, combine the spinach, banana, almond milk, and chia seeds. Blend until smooth.
2. Pour the mixture into a bowl.
3. Top with sliced almonds and mixed berries (if desired).
4. Enjoy your magnesium-packed smoothie bowl!

Tip: Customize with your favorite fruits or a spoonful of nut butter for added flavor.

Almond-Crusted Salmon

Ingredients:

- 4 salmon fillets
- 1 cup crushed almonds
- 2 tablespoons olive oil
- 1 teaspoon garlic powder
- Salt and pepper to taste
- 2 cups Swiss chard, sautéed

Instructions:

1. Preheat oven to 375°F (190°C).
2. In a shallow dish, mix together crushed almonds, olive oil, garlic powder, salt and pepper.
3. Coat both sides of the salmon fillets in the almond mixture.
4. Place salmon on a greased baking sheet and bake for 12-15 minutes until flaky.
5. Serve with sautéed Swiss chard for an extra boost of magnesium!

Tip: Add a squeeze of lemon juice before serving for extra zest.

Quinoa Black Bean Salad

Ingredients:

- 1 cup of cooked quinoa
- 1 can (15 oz) of black beans, rinsed and drained
- 1 cup of cherry tomatoes, cut in half
- 1 avocado, chopped
- 1/4 cup of lime juice
- Salt and pepper to your liking

Instructions:

1. Mix the cooked quinoa, black beans, cherry tomatoes, and avocado together in a large bowl.
2. Drizzle with lime juice and toss to coat.
3. Add salt and pepper according to your taste preferences.
4. Enjoy this flavorful and magnesium-rich salad as a side dish or main course!

Tip: Prepare in advance for meal prep and store in an airtight container.

Chia Seed Pudding

Ingredients:

- 1/4 cup chia seeds
- 1 cup almond milk
- 1 teaspoon vanilla extract
- 1 banana, sliced
- 1 teaspoon cinnamon

Instructions:

1. In a jar or container, mix together chia seeds, almond milk, and vanilla extract.
2. Cover and refrigerate for at least 4 hours or overnight.
3. When ready to serve, top with sliced banana and sprinkle with cinnamon.
4. This creamy and nutritious pudding is loaded with magnesium from the chia seeds and almonds!

Tip: Experiment with different toppings such as berries, nuts, or shredded coconut.

Dark Chocolate Almond Bark

Ingredients:

- 1 cup dark chocolate chips
- 1 cup whole almonds

Instructions:

1. Melt dark chocolate chips in a microwave-safe bowl or double boiler.
2. Spread almonds on a baking sheet lined with parchment paper.
3. Pour melted chocolate over almonds and spread evenly.
4. Allow to cool and set, then break into pieces.

Tip: Store in an airtight container for a quick snack.

Lentil and Spinach Soup

Ingredients:

- 1 cup lentils
- 4 cups vegetable broth
- 2 cups fresh spinach leaves
- 1 cup diced carrots
- 1 onion, chopped
- 2 cloves garlic, minced

Instructions:

1. In a large pot, sauté onion and garlic until fragrant.
2. Add lentils, broth, and carrots. Bring to a boil, then simmer for 30 minutes.
3. Stir in spinach and cook until wilted.
4. Season with salt and pepper to taste before serving.

Tip: Pair with crusty bread for a complete meal.

Avocado and Pumpkin Seed Toast

Ingredients:

- 4 slices whole-grain bread
- 2 ripe avocados
- 1/4 cup pumpkin seeds
- Salt and pepper to taste

Instructions:

1. Toast bread slices until golden brown.
2. Mash avocados and spread them evenly on each slice.
3. Sprinkle with pumpkin seeds, salt, and pepper before serving.

Tip: Add sliced tomatoes or a poached egg for extra nutrition.

Brown Rice and Tofu Stir-Fry

Ingredients:

- 1 cup cooked brown rice
- 1 block of firm tofu, cubed
- 1 cup broccoli florets
- 1 red bell pepper, sliced
- 2 tablespoons soy sauce
- 1 tablespoon sesame seeds

Instructions:

1. In a large pan, cook tofu until golden.
2. Add broccoli and bell pepper, stir-frying until tender.
3. Mix in cooked brown rice and soy sauce, tossing to combine.
4. Sprinkle with sesame seeds before serving.

Tip: Add your favorite vegetables for variety.

Baked Sweet Potatoes with Black Beans

Ingredients:

- 2 large sweet potatoes
- 1 can (15 oz) black beans, rinsed and drained
- 1/2 cup Greek yogurt
- Salt, pepper, and cumin to taste

Instructions:

1. Preheat oven to 400°F and pierce sweet potatoes with a fork.
2. Place sweet potatoes on a baking sheet and bake for 45 minutes, or until tender.
3. In a separate bowl, mix black beans, Greek yogurt, salt, pepper, and cumin.
4. Top each sweet potato with the bean mixture before serving.

Tip: Garnish with fresh cilantro for added flavor.

Kale and Almond Salad

Ingredients:

- 4 cups kale, chopped
- 1/4 cup olive oil
- 1 lemon, juiced
- 1/2 cup sliced almonds
- 1/4 cup crumbled feta cheese

Instructions:

1. In a large mixing bowl, massage kale with olive oil and lemon juice until the leaves are tender.
2. Add sliced almonds and feta cheese, tossing to combine.
3. Serve as a side dish or add protein, such as grilled chicken, for a complete meal.

Tip: Add dried cranberries or apple slices for sweetness.

Almond and Banana Oatmeal

Ingredients:

- 1 cup rolled oats
- 2 cups almond milk
- 1 ripe banana, sliced
- 2 tablespoons almond butter
- 1 tablespoon chia seeds
- 1 teaspoon cinnamon
- 1 tablespoon honey or maple syrup (optional)

Instructions:

1. In a saucepan, combine the oats and almond milk. Bring to a boil, then reduce heat and simmer for about 5 minutes, stirring occasionally.
2. Stir in the almond butter, chia seeds, and cinnamon. Continue to cook until the oatmeal reaches your desired consistency.
3. Remove from heat and top with banana slices. Drizzle with honey or maple syrup if desired.
4. Serve warm and enjoy your magnesium-packed breakfast.

Quinoa and Kale Stuffed Peppers

Ingredients:

- 4 large bell peppers, halved and seeds removed
- 1 cup cooked quinoa
- 2 cups chopped kale
- 1 can (15 oz) black beans, drained and rinsed
- 1 cup corn kernels (fresh or frozen)
- 1 teaspoon cumin
- 1 teaspoon paprika
- Salt and pepper to taste

Instructions:

1. Preheat oven to 375°F (190°C).
2. Place halved bell peppers in a baking dish, cut side up.
3. In a large bowl, mix together the quinoa, kale, black beans, corn, cumin, paprika, salt, and pepper.
4. Stuff each pepper half with the quinoa mixture.
5. Cover with foil and bake for 25-30 minutes, until the peppers are tender.
6. Serve hot, garnished with fresh herbs if desired.

Spinach and Pumpkin Seed Pesto Pasta

Ingredients:

- 12 oz whole wheat pasta
- 2 cups fresh spinach
- 1/2 cup pumpkin seeds
- 1/4 cup grated Parmesan cheese
- 2 cloves garlic
- 1/4 cup olive oil
- Salt and pepper to taste
- Juice of half a lemon

Instructions:

1. Cook pasta according to package instructions. Drain and set aside.
2. In a food processor, blend together spinach, pumpkin seeds, Parmesan cheese, garlic, olive oil, lemon juice, salt, and pepper until smooth.
3. Toss the cooked pasta with the spinach pesto until well coated.
4. Serve immediately, garnished with additional Parmesan cheese and pumpkin seeds if desired.

Lentil and Avocado Wrap

Ingredients:

- 1 cup cooked lentils
- 1 ripe avocado, sliced
- 1 cup shredded lettuce
- 1/2 cup grated carrot
- 1/2 cup sliced cucumber
- 4 whole grain wraps
- 2 tablespoons hummus

Instructions:

1. Lay out the whole-grain wraps on a flat surface.
2. Spread 1/2 tablespoon of hummus onto each wrap, leaving a small border around the edges.
3. Divide cooked lentils evenly among the wraps, spreading them down the center of each wrap.
4. Top with sliced avocado, shredded lettuce, grated carrot, and sliced cucumber.
5. Roll up each wrap tightly and slice in half before serving.
6. Serve cold or warm in a panini press for a crispy exterior.

Dark Chocolate and Nut Clusters

Ingredients:

- 1 cup dark chocolate chips
- 1/2 cup almonds
- 1/2 cup walnuts
- 1/2 cup sunflower seeds
- Sea salt (optional)

Instructions:

1. Melt the dark chocolate chips in a microwave-safe bowl or using a double boiler.
2. Stir in the almonds, walnuts, and sunflower seeds until well coated.
3. Drop spoonfuls of the mixture onto a baking sheet lined with parchment paper.
4. Sprinkle with sea salt if desired.
5. Let the clusters set at room temperature or refrigerate until firm.
6. Store in an airtight container and enjoy it as a snack or dessert.

Incorporating these magnesium-rich recipes into your daily diet can significantly enhance your overall health and wellness. Magnesium is an essential mineral that supports numerous bodily functions, including muscle and nerve activity, bone health, and energy production. By trying these delicious and versatile dishes, you'll not only boost your magnesium intake but also enjoy a wide range of flavors and textures.

Each recipe is designed for ease of preparation, making it simple to integrate nutritious meals into even the busiest of routines. Embrace the diversity of magnesium-rich foods and elevate your culinary experience while nourishing your body.

CONCLUSION

As you reach the end of this in-depth exploration of magnesium and its vital role in health, it's clear that understanding and incorporating this mineral into your wellness routine can significantly enhance your quality of life. We've delved into the myriad ways magnesium supports your body, from facilitating over 300 biochemical reactions to boosting energy, improving sleep, and promoting overall well-being.

Magnesium's importance in energy production cannot be overstated. By stabilizing ATP, the energy currency of the cell, magnesium helps you maintain vitality and reduce fatigue. This means more energy for your daily activities and a greater zest for life. Furthermore, magnesium supports mental health by stabilizing mood and reducing stress, which can lead to a more balanced emotional state and improved resilience against life's challenges.

When it comes to incorporating magnesium into your daily life, you have a variety of options. The different forms of magnesium, such as citrate, oxide, and glycinate, each offer unique benefits. It's important to select the form that aligns with your specific health goals, whether it's improving sleep, enhancing athletic performance, or supporting heart health. Consulting a healthcare provider is crucial here; they can offer personalized guidance to help you choose the right form and dosage.

In addition to supplements, integrating magnesium-rich foods into your diet is an excellent way to boost your intake naturally. Foods like leafy greens, nuts, seeds, and whole grains are not only rich in magnesium but also offer a range of other nutrients that contribute to your overall nutritional profile. By consistently including these foods in your meals, you can maintain adequate magnesium levels and enjoy the accompanying health benefits.

Lifestyle changes can further enhance how effectively your body absorbs magnesium. Reducing your intake of caffeine and alcohol, managing stress through techniques like yoga or meditation, and ensuring you get enough vitamin D are all strategies that can improve magnesium absorption. Staying hydrated is another simple yet effective habit that supports digestion and mineral uptake, contributing to your overall health.

As you embark on this journey with magnesium, remain attentive to how your body responds. Track changes in your energy levels, sleep quality, and mood to gauge the impact of magnesium on your well-being. Keep an open line of communication with your healthcare provider to refine your approach, especially if you encounter any adverse effects or have questions about your supplementation regimen.

Your commitment to enhancing your health through magnesium is a positive step towards a more vibrant, healthier life. By making magnesium a regular part of your wellness routine, you can unlock new levels of energy, resilience, and overall well-being. Thank you for dedicating your time to this guide and for taking proactive steps towards better health.

As you move forward, embrace the diverse world of magnesium-rich foods, explore the variety of supplements available, and enjoy the process of discovering what works best for you. With consistency, informed choices, and patience, you'll soon experience the transformative power of magnesium in your daily life.

FAQS

What are the different forms of magnesium, and which one should I choose?

Magnesium comes in various forms, including magnesium citrate, oxide, glycinate, and malate. Each form has unique properties and absorption rates. For example, magnesium citrate is known for its high absorption and is often used for digestive health, while magnesium glycinate is gentle on the stomach and may aid in improving sleep quality. It's important to select the form that aligns with your health goals and consult a healthcare provider for personalized recommendations.

What are the potential side effects of magnesium supplementation?

While magnesium is generally safe, taking large doses can lead to digestive issues such as diarrhea, nausea, or abdominal cramping. In rare cases, excessive magnesium can cause more serious symptoms like irregular heartbeats or low blood pressure. It's crucial to follow recommended dosages and consult with a healthcare provider to avoid adverse effects.

What are some good dietary sources of magnesium?

Magnesium-rich foods are essential for maintaining overall health and well-being. These include leafy greens, such as spinach and kale, which are packed with vitamins and minerals in addition to magnesium. Nuts, particularly almonds and cashews, provide not only magnesium but also healthy fats and protein, making them a great snack option.

Seeds like pumpkin seeds are another excellent source, offering a crunchy texture and versatility in dishes. Whole grains, such as quinoa and brown rice, are not only rich in magnesium but also provide fiber, which aids in digestion. Lastly, legumes like black beans are a fantastic addition, as they are high in protein and other nutrients. Including a diverse array of these foods in your diet can help maintain adequate magnesium levels naturally, supporting muscle function, energy production, and overall health.

How does magnesium benefit my overall health?

Magnesium supports over 300 biochemical reactions in the body, contributing to energy production, muscle function, and nerve health. It also helps regulate mood, supports heart health, and promotes better sleep. Adequate magnesium levels can enhance vitality, reduce stress, and improve overall well-being.

Can magnesium help with sleep and relaxation?

Yes, magnesium is well-known for its calming effects on the nervous system, playing a crucial role in promoting mental well-being. This essential mineral helps regulate the production of melatonin, which is the hormone responsible for managing sleep-wake cycles. By ensuring that melatonin levels remain balanced, magnesium can facilitate a smoother transition into sleep.

Additionally, it promotes relaxation by aiding in the reduction of stress and anxiety levels, making it easier for individuals to not only fall asleep but also enjoy deeper, more restorative sleep stages. Furthermore, adequate magnesium intake can contribute to improved overall sleep quality, leading to enhanced daily functioning and mood stability.

How can I incorporate magnesium into my daily routine?

To effectively incorporate magnesium into your routine, consider adding magnesium-rich foods to your diet, such as leafy greens, nuts, seeds, whole grains, and legumes. These foods not only provide magnesium but also come packed with other essential nutrients that support overall health. Additionally, when choosing a magnesium supplement, look for one that aligns with your specific health goals, whether it's for muscle recovery, improved sleep, or enhanced relaxation.

Consistency is crucial for maximizing benefits, so try to take your magnesium supplement at the same time each day to build a habit. Additionally, lifestyle changes can greatly improve magnesium absorption. For example, cutting back on caffeine and alcohol can prevent magnesium depletion, while managing stress through mindfulness, yoga, or regular exercise can enhance your body's ability to absorb this essential mineral. By making these adjustments, you can ensure your body gets the magnesium it needs for optimal function.

Should I consult a healthcare provider before taking magnesium supplements?

Absolutely. Consulting a healthcare provider is essential, especially if you have existing health conditions or are taking medications that might interact with magnesium supplements. Some medications, such as certain antibiotics or diuretics, can have their effectiveness altered by magnesium, making professional guidance crucial.

A healthcare professional can offer personalized advice tailored to your specific health profile, including the appropriate form of magnesium, such as magnesium citrate or magnesium glycinate, and the right dosage to suit your individual needs. This ensures that your supplementation is both safe and effective, helping you achieve optimal health without unnecessary risks.

RESOURCES AND HELPFUL LINKS

Office of Dietary Supplements - magnesium. (n.d.). https://ods.od.nih.gov/factsheets/Magnesium-HealthProfessional/

Yablon, L. A., & Mauskop, A. (2011). *Magnesium in headache.* Magnesium in the Central Nervous System - NCBI Bookshelf. https://www.ncbi.nlm.nih.gov/books/NBK507271/#:~:text=Research%20on%20magnesium%20has%20found,particularly%20in%20certain%20patient%20subsets.

Magnesium, a treatment for leg cramps? (2014, February 27). NPS MedicineWise. https://www.nps.org.au/news/magnesium-a-treatment-for-leg-cramps#:~:text=Since%20magnesium%20plays%20a%20role,may%20predispose%20to%20muscle%20cramps.&text=Thus%20magnesium%20supplements%20are%20often%20recommended%20to%20prevent%20cramps.

Moabedi, M., Aliakbari, M., Erfanian, S., & Milajerdi, A. (2023). Magnesium supplementation beneficially affects depression in adults with depressive disorder: a systematic review and meta-analysis of randomized clinical trials. *Frontiers in Psychiatry, 14.* https://doi.org/10.3389/fpsyt.2023.1333261

Geng, C. (2023, August 1). *Does magnesium help you sleep?* https://www.medicalnewstoday.com/articles/magnesium-for-sleep#:~:text=Magnesium%20and%20melatonin%20promote%20sleep,with%20a%20disrupted%20circadian%20rhythm.

Isy. (2024, May 9). Magnesium for athletes - Speeding up recovery ! | Elite Performance Therapy. *Coaching & Sports Massage*. https://elite-performance-therapy.com/magnesium-for-athletes-speeding-up-recovery/

Jade, C. (2024, September 25). *Top 10 magnesium rich recipes*. Cooking With Jade. https://cookingwithjade.com/top-10-magnesium-rich-recipes/?srsltid=AfmBOopn7nN4CkkeAgSRIEjlxUOCUIus2tIIoxIOTvz_e6ntSES7LaIT

Eat This Much, Inc. (n.d.). *Eat This Much, your personal diet assistant*. Eat This Much. https://www.eatthismuch.com/food/browse/high-magnesium-recipes/?q=&type=recipe&order_by=-magnesium&show_nutrient=magnesium

Itn, T. (2018, November 19). *The Beginner's Guide To Magnesium: What It Is, Why We Need It, And How To Get It*. Institute of Transformational Nutrition | Health Coach Certification Program. https://transformationalnutrition.com/blog/science-of-nutrition/beginners-guide-magnesium/

www.ingramcontent.com/pod-product-compliance
Lightning Source LLC
LaVergne TN
LVHW052000060526
838201LV00059B/3752